The Mummy

Other titles in the Monsters and Mythical Creatures series include:

Aliens
Cyclops
Demons
Dragons
Frankenstein
Goblins
Medusa
Trolls
Water Monsters
Zombies

Monsters
and Mythical Creatures

The Mummy

David Robson

ReferencePoint
Press®

San Diego, CA

© 2012 ReferencePoint Press, Inc.
Printed in the United States

For more information, contact:
ReferencePoint Press, Inc.
PO Box 27779
San Diego, CA 92198
www. ReferencePointPress.com

LIBRARY OF CONGRESS CATALOGING-IN-PUBLICATION DATA

Robson, David, 1966–
The mummy / by David Robson.
    p. cm. — (Monsters and mythical creatures)
Includes bibliographical references and index.
ISBN-13: 978-1-60152-182-8 (hardback)
ISBN-10: 1-60152-182-0 (hardback)
1. Mummies. I. Title.
GN293.R62 2012
393'.3—dc23
                                                          2011022437

Contents

Death to Life

Each Halloween, children in the United States and at least 14 other countries brave the autumn chill. Dressed as ghouls, witches, or the latest pop sensation, these trick-or-treaters traipse from house to house in search of free candy. School pageants and parades bring out still more fantastic figures: ninjas, sports stars, and comic book characters. But while costumed creations often vary from year to year, three remain staples: Dracula, Frankenstein's monster, and the mummy.

What connects the three classic monsters is death. Dracula, a vampire, is one of the undead. He prowls the night hiding behind his black cape and looking for fresh blood to drink. In the original story, Frankenstein's monster is a half-rotted corpse brought back to life. In his reanimated state he is a huge, green, bolt-necked man-child. The mummy, too, once walked among the living.

Mummy Mystique

In the pantheon of monsters, the Egyptian mummy occupies a vital and unique place. Thousands of years ago, in the Nile Valley, some of the first mummies came into being—first by accident and later on purpose. Most mummified Egyptians were of royal birth, and the solemn high priests that prepared them for the next world took time and care to make the journey into the afterlife a safe and successful one. In fact, the mummy's journey from death to life was the end result of months or even years of preparation.

For contemporary horror enthusiasts, the mummy's ancient and exotic heritage is part of its creepy charm. Separated from its religious origins by millennia, the image of the mummy retains its mystery but is well known enough to be used as the butt of jokes or as the cheesy villain in Saturday morning cartoons. The mummy tale is so well known, in fact, that most schoolchildren could recite it by heart: A group of nerdy archaeologists or daft teenagers open the long-closed tomb of a slumbering Egyptian pharaoh. Foolishly, one of them pockets a glittering amulet or removes a sarcophagus from its musty burial chamber. Ever so slowly, the mummy awakens. Those in the room usually do not notice as the dried-out dead body opens one eye, then the other, before lifting its arms, moving its legs, and rising from its coffin, its linen bandages trailing behind it.

Wrapped in soiled, crumbling strips of linen, actor Lon Chaney Jr. strangles his victim in the 1944 film The Mummy's Ghost. *Movie mummies have traditionally been lumbering, inarticulate, and murderous.*

Like Frankenstein's monster, the mummy typically appears as a lumbering, inarticulate marauder. Rather than voice its murderous, vengeful desires, it grunts and moans. But what the mummy lacks in conversational abilities it makes up for in seismic strength. It carefully watches the intruders before sneaking up on them, gingerly wrapping its bare, sandpapery hands around their throats and strangling the interlopers to death.

The Mummy in Our Midst

For nearly a century, Hollywood has exploited this idea of the mummy legends to attract people to the movie theater. And it has worked. The earliest films were mostly inspired by one of the greatest archaeological discoveries of the twentieth century, the tomb of King Tutankhamun. Before that, an all-consuming fascination with all things mummy and a belief in their healing powers led to the destruction of scores of the precious artifacts. Equally misunderstood or forgotten are the various curses and myths of mummy lore. And while scientific evidence has proved these supposed supernatural happenings to be little more than superstition, contemporary audiences still enjoy screaming over a good, old-fashioned mummy story.

> ## Did You Know?
>
> The word "mummy" comes from the Arabic word for bitumen: *mumya*. Bitumen is a black sticky mixture of naturally-occurring liquids. Over time, the word *mumya* evolved into the name we recognize today: mummy.

In the twenty-first century, the mummy as monster has appeared on everything from cereal boxes to TV commercials to soap. Indeed, the mummy's bandaged body rises from the tomb over and over and, in the process, has become an unmistakable cultural icon, known by all ages. The mummy, it appears, is here to stay.

Chapter 1

The Mummy as Monster

For the ancient Egyptians, the mummification of a dead body was a sacred ritual. For contemporary audiences, the mummy is less sacred than scary. Swaddled in layers of fabric, the mummy rises from its tomb to avenge those foolish enough to disturb it. Modern versions of the murderous mummy often add the element of ancient love torn apart by the passing millennia. Although mummies have been shown by scientists to be thousands of years old, the concept of the mummy as monster is a twentieth-century invention. In the recent past, moviemakers, authors, and artists looking for inspiration often looked to North Africa and the rich and mysterious culture that populated the Nile Valley. Part reality, part invention, the image of the murderous mummy first took root in the popular imagination upon the release of one of the most legendary horror films of all time.

Karloff's Mummy

By 1932 Universal Pictures had established itself as the premier maker of monster movies in Hollywood. Only a year before, Universal had released two box office hits, *Dracula* and *Frankenstein*. The latter film had featured a star-making performance by British character actor Boris Karloff. Theater owners had reported audience members shrieking in horror as Karloff's cadaverous "creature" appeared onscreen for the first time. Yet Karloff's portrayal of the

Mummification was a sacred ritual in ancient Egyptian culture, but mummies, such as this one found in ancient Egypt, have often been portrayed in movies as evil or lovelorn and possessing supernatural powers.

lumbering and feeble-minded monster remained in viewers' minds long after the movie ended. Classically trained, Karloff was nonetheless quickly typecast, and less than a year after *Frankenstein* he was again before the cameras in a role to die for.

Production on the film that became *The Mummy* began in 1931. Producer Carl Laemmle Jr. hired veteran story editor Richard Shayer to find a novel or other literary basis for another work of horror. Laemmle believed that *Dracula* and *Frankenstein* owed much of their success to their pedigree as serious literature. But unlike those two monster pictures, the mummy movie would be based on an Italian legend. Working with screenwriter Nina Wilcox Putnam, Shayer developed a storyline based on the legend of an eighteenth-century Italian who told people he was an alchemist—someone with the magical ability to make gold from base metals. The alchemist also became popular in society as a mystic. The resulting story, called *Cagliostro*, seemed a worthwhile vehicle for Karloff and would be set in San Francisco, California.

Soon after, Laemmle hired playwright John L. Balderston, who had worked on the scripts for *Dracula* and *Frankenstein*, to write the screenplay. As a journalist, Balderston had spent time in Egypt and decided to turn *Cagliostro* into a mummy picture to be set, naturally, in North Africa. The first draft of Balderston's screenplay was titled *Imhotep*, after an Egyptian architect who, according to legend, designed the first pyramid. Another working title, *King of the Dead*, was also used in the early stages of production. Balderston also added a new theme to the Putnam and Shayer version: love transcending centuries.

Production Begins

With a script in place, a budget of approximately $196,000, and the shooting dates fast approaching, Laemmle hired cinematographer

Karl Freund to direct the film. Known for his ability to move the typically stationary camera in exciting new ways, Freund appeared to be the perfect choice to take the director's chair. Filming of *The Mummy*, its new name, began in September 1932 and was scheduled to last for three weeks.

The mummy's makeup was an integral part of the film, and for it, designer Jack Pierce created an elaborate and time-consuming process. The process took eight hours to complete each day before the cameras rolled. In these early days of cinema, makeup techniques were primitive but effective. Using an adhesive called spirit gum and wads of Egyptian cotton, Pierce stretched Karloff's skin, painted a layer of collodion—a syrup-like substance—onto the actor's skin, and added another layer of sticky spirit gum or collodion. Once dried, the layers were removed and the wrinkle effect that Pierce was after took hold. "Physical exhaustion was nothing compared to the nervous exhaustion I suffered,"[1] Karloff said later about the lengthy makeup process for the movie.

According to Oscar-winning makeup artist Rick Baker, the combination of Pierce's technique and Karloff's appearance made the mummy's appearance in the film unforgettable.

> **Did You Know?**
>
> The name "Ardath Bey," Karloff's character in *The Mummy*, is an anagram of "Death by Ra." Ra was the Egyptian sun god.

"I think what made *The Mummy* make-up work was Karloff and Karloff's face," says Baker. "He had this great bone structure for it, and his performance . . . was very subtle but it was frightening."[2]

Less subtle but equally unnerving were the opening moments of Karl Freund's film, which begins with the following words: "This is the scroll of Thoth. Herein are set down the magic words by which Isis raised Osiris from the dead."[3] The story itself opens in 1921 as a team of British archaeologists uncovers the 3,700-year-old mummy of Imhotep. In perhaps the movie's most famous sequence, a young archaeologist unwisely opens the scroll of Thoth and is driven to

William Henry Pratt's Alter Ego

The man who would become one of the greatest screen horror icons was born William Henry Pratt in London, England, on November 23, 1887. His father, Edward, worked as a customs commissioner. Young William attended London University and had aspirations to become a diplomat, but during his time at college he fell in with a group of actors, which changed his life forever. In 1909 he immigrated to Canada and found work in an Ontario touring company. It was at this time that he took the stage name Boris Karloff. Although explanations differ, Karloff suggested he took the name "Boris" because of its foreign and exotic sounds; "Karloff," he claimed, was an old family name.

For more than a decade the actor performed in plays across North America and eventually found himself in Hollywood. There, he played bit roles in a string of silent movies beginning in 1920 and made ends meet by driving a truck part-time. Finally, in 1931 he landed the part of the creature in *Frankenstein*. The role changed his life and cinema history. Afterward, he starred in dozens of movies but often found himself typecast as villainous characters.

Karloff's personal life was complicated and often unhappy. He married six times over the course of his life. Still, costars were most often struck by Karloff's kindness and gentle manner. His costar Zita Johann retained fond memories of Karloff from *The Mummy* shoot: "Boris Karloff was really, truly a great gentleman," she said. "There was in Karloff a hidden sorrow that I sensed and respected—a deep, deep thing. Still, whatever that may have been, there was a true respect between us as actors."

Quoted in Gregory William Mank, *Bela Lugosi and Boris Karloff: The Expanded Story of a Haunting Collaboration*. Jefferson, NC: McFarland, 2009, p. 128.

insanity when the mummy slowly opens its eyes, moves its ancient limbs, and escapes.

Ten years later the head archaeologist, Sir Joseph Whemple, returns with his son Frank. The escaped mummy is now disguised as a mysterious, crinkly-skinned Egyptian named Ardath Bey, also played by Karloff. Bey helps the expedition uncover the tomb of his ancient love. He then uses his mystic powers to hasten the reincarnation of his lost love in the form of Helen Grosvenor. Whemple mysteriously dies when he interferes. His son Frank has fallen in love with Helen, and with the help of Egyptologist Dr. Muller, the two men attempt to discover the key to Bey's powers and break the spell he has put on Helen.

Release and Reception

The Mummy was released in December 1932. Hoping to capitalize on Karloff's newly minted *Frankenstein*-fueled stardom, Universal promoted him as "KARLOFF the Uncanny."[4] In January 1933 the film opened at the RKO Mayfair Theatre in New York City. Box office business was modest, as the film received mixed reviews. While praised in the *Los Angeles Times*, the *New York Times* gave *The Mummy* a tepid review. The newspaper praised the movie's photography and two of its scenes but called the film "costume melodrama for the children."[5] Its lead actor fared no better: "Mr. Karloff acts with the restraint natural to a man whose face is hidden behind synthetic wrinkles."[6]

In 1999, contemporary critic Roger Ebert called Karloff's performance "strangely poignant" and noted that "the 1932 movie contains no violence to speak of; there's hardly any action, indeed, and the chills come through slow realizations (hey, did that mummy move?)."[7] Ebert's evaluation echoes the film's status as one of the legendary horror movies of all time. The film's enduring influence and status as a classic was reinforced in 1997, when an unidentified private collector paid $453,500 for an original poster from *The Mummy*. This high price beat the previous record—$198,000—for the sale of a movie poster.

The Mummy forever popularized the image of the bandage-clad corpse stalking the streets of Cairo. But its inspiration was a startling discovery made ten years earlier. As a young journalist, Balderston had covered that story, but so had newspapers across the world.

Precious Objects Discovered

In the late nineteenth century, Europeans and Americans were captivated by Egypt and its culture. Stories from antiquity told of an advanced civilization both familiar and mysterious. And buried deep in the desert sands were the mummified bodies of pharaohs, or kings. By the dawn of the twentieth century, many scholars and archaeologists argued that few ancient tombs were yet to be discovered.

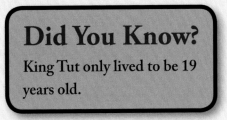

Did You Know?
King Tut only lived to be 19 years old.

The great finds of the age had been made; Egyptian relics were now housed in museums or in private collections. Theodore M. Davis refused to believe them.

Davis was an American businessman with a deep-seated interest in finding yet-to-be-discovered royal tombs. During excavations, Davis came upon a collection, or cache, of intriguing funerary pieces. These valuable objects included cups, bowls, furniture, caskets, mummies, and embalming materials. The clay seal that Davis found affixed to many of these objects bore the mark of King Tutankhamun, or King Tut, a pharaoh who ruled Egypt from 1333 to 1323 BC. Davis and others believed the cache had been buried in another known tomb by tomb robbers. This minor but encouraging discovery led Davis to believe that Tut's tomb remained undisturbed in the Valley of the Kings, a long stretch of desert near Luxor, Egypt, that is the final resting place of at least 63 pharaohs and other high-ranking officials.

A few years later, in 1907, more objects were found in a pit near Cairo by other archaeologists. Again, royal seals of Tut were found on many of them. Also in this cache were linen bags, broken pottery, and natron, a powdery compound used in the mummification process. Unfortunately, the clues that could have led to unearthing

Tut's tomb were overlooked, and the objects were sent to New York City for further study. Likewise, Davis failed to take seriously a cup with Tut's name on it and fragments of gold foil with the names Tutankhamun and Ankhesenamun, his wife, written on them. Frustrated and losing any hope that a pristine tomb might be found, Davis lost interest. Young Howard Carter, on the other hand, was certain Tut's tomb could be found in the Valley of the Kings.

Howard Carter and King Tut

The British-born Carter had started his Egyptian sojourn at the age of 17 in 1891, hiring himself out as a sketch artist. By day he copied wall scenes and inscriptions found inside the burial vaults. By night he dreamed of making his own fantastic discoveries. It was Carter's practical skills that caught the eye of British officials in Cairo. In

One of the legendary horror films of all time, The Mummy, starred Boris Karloff in the title role. The 1932 film, promoted in this movie poster, popularized the image of the bandage-clad corpse stalking the streets of Egypt's cities.

and now **KARLOFF**
THE UNCANNY
as **"MUMMY"**
It comes to Life!
A UNIVERSAL PICTURE *presented by* CARL LAEMMLE
ZITA JOHANN DAVID MANNERS EDWARD VAN SLOAN *Story by* NINA WILCOX PUTNAM *and* RICHARD SCHAYER — ARTHUR BYRON *directed by* KARL FREUND *produced by* CARL LAEMMLE

1899 he was appointed inspector-general of monuments in Upper Egypt. The work, though, kept him from his true passion: the dig. In 1905 he resigned from his government position; two years later he was hired by George Edward Stanhope Molyneux Herbert, the fifth Earl of Carnarvon. Lord Carnarvon, as he was commonly known, had taken up Egyptian antiquities as a hobby after a car accident forced him into early retirement.

Now Carnarvon put his faith in Carter, despite the many other explorers convinced that King Tut's tomb did not exist or was buried forever beneath the dry desert sands. Carter's work was preempted by the First World War, which raged from 1914 to 1918. One year before the war ended, in 1917, Carter and Carnarvon commenced a dig in the Valley of the Kings. Unlike Davis, the artifacts already found that bore Tut's emblem convinced Carter that the task of unearthing the tomb was not

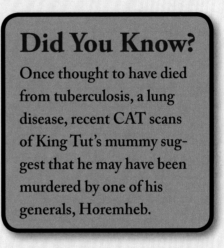

Did You Know?

Once thought to have died from tuberculosis, a lung disease, recent CAT scans of King Tut's mummy suggest that he may have been murdered by one of his generals, Horemheb.

impossible. Like a twentieth-century Sherlock Holmes, Carter deduced that since the objects had been found near the tomb of Pharaoh Ramses VI, he would begin digging there and drill to the bedrock, if necessary. Using local workers, Carter began the laborious task of removing layers of sand and sediment around the foot of Ramses's tomb.

For five years during the digging season, Carter and his small army of Egyptians displaced tons of earth, discovering only 13 calcite jars and a group of ancient huts used by workmen 3,000 years earlier. Any clue as to the whereabouts of Tut's tomb remained hidden. Carnarvon, like so many others before him, decided to give up the apparently fruitless search. Carter begged his patron to support him for one more digging season and, after much cajoling, Carnarvon agreed. But this would be Carter's last chance.

One More Try

At the first opportunity, Carter had his workers return to the ancient work huts. Working more by instinct than intellect, Carter ordered his men to dig beneath the huts. The date was November 1, 1922. For three more days the laborers performed the backbreaking work of hauling cartloads of sand to the surface. On that fourth day of digging, one of the workers found a step cut into the rock. Long buried by sand and clotted soil, the step provided Carter and his team hope that they were onto something.

By afternoon on November 5, as the sun dipped behind the pyramids, the workers had dug deeply enough to reveal 12 steps descending still farther into the sand. Also apparent was the top portion of a huge doorway. Carter inspected the door for seals that might identify his find. He found the seals but could not read the worn symbols. What he could see from the decor and embellishments was that it was a royal tomb. "The design was certainly of the Eighteenth Dynasty," Carter later wrote. "Could it be the tomb of a noble buried here by royal consent? Was it a royal cache, a hiding-place to which a mummy and its equipment had been removed for safety? Or was it actually the tomb of the king for whom I had spent so many years in search?"[8]

In the weeks to come, Carter would realize the value of his find. After waiting three weeks for the arrival of Carnarvon and his daughter, Lady Evelyn Herbert, from Europe, Carter resumed his work. After fully exposing the ancient doorway, he could now clearly read the name of Tutankhamun on the royal seals. He peered through a hole into the main chamber:

"At first I could see nothing," Carter later wrote, "the hot air escaping from the chamber causing the candle flame to flicker, but presently, as my eyes grew accustomed to the light, details of the room within emerged slowly from the mist, strange animals, statues, and gold—everywhere the glint of gold."[9]

This magical moment, earned after years of fruitless searching, marked the beginning of Carter's discovery, the contents of which would take years to catalog. The unveiling of Tut's tomb cre-

Delicate Treasure Trove

By the time Howard Carter uncovered King Tutankhamun's tomb in 1922, it had most likely already been plundered twice by ancient robbers. Yet the scale of what remained was still enormous. Thousands of items crowded at least two main rooms; Carter realized he could not catalog all of the contents by himself. Thus, he hired more than a dozen specialists. At the outset, each item from the tomb was photographed with and without a number for ordering purposes. Then, a sketch of individual pieces and a description was created. The item was then marked on a ground plan, so those reading the plan later would understand its original location.

The fragility of the artifacts prompted Carter and his staff to work carefully and with delicacy. "Clearing the objects from the Antechamber was like playing a gigantic game of spillikins," writes Carter. "In some cases they were so inextricably tangled that an elaborate system of props and supports had to be devised to hold one object or group of objects in place while another was being removed. At such times life was a nightmare." A celluloid spray was applied to the items, which kept the objects from falling apart. For final removal from the tomb, technicians wrapped the antiquities in gauze or linen for protection and placed them on stretchers. As the full stretchers were carried from the dark recesses of the humid tomb, they were greeted with cheers by hundreds of gathered onlookers.

Howard Carter and A.C. Mace, *Tomb of Tutankhamen*. New York: Kessinger, 2003, p. 177.

ated a worldwide frenzy: Mummy lust was at its peak. But it was what happened in the aftermath of the discovery that turned the nineteenth-century image of the mummy into a twentieth-century monster.

The Curse

Standing near the doorway in one of the tomb's burial chambers stood two life-size statues of the dead pharaoh. Made of wood and standing on reed mats, they had likely stood in the young king's palace during his lifetime. The statues themselves wore sandals made of solid gold and golden crowns with a slithery cobra in each, representing kingly power.

According to a *New York Times* report from the time, the day of the discovery brought with it a strange incident. During that year of digging, Carter had brought a canary to Egypt with him. He kept it in a cage outside on the veranda. At an evening dinner party to celebrate the find, a sudden shriek was heard. Carter and his guests dashed outside to see a cobra attacking the canary. Carter killed the snake, but too late; the canary was dead. The house staff, made up of Egyptians, took the bird's death as an omen. "The incident made an impression on the native staff who regard it as a warning from the spirit of the departed king against further intrusion on the privacy of his tomb,"[10] wrote the *Times* reporter. For decades, rumors of ancient curses circulated among the archaeologists in Egypt. Like most of his scientific colleagues, Carter was highly skeptical of such superstition. Then, in early 1923 Carnarvon suffered a mosquito bite on his left cheek. As it was healing, Carnarvon reopened the bite when he cut himself shaving. This seemingly innocuous event would prove serious indeed.

> ## Did You Know?
>
> Although Howard Carter did not believe in curses, in a May 1926 diary entry he recorded seeing a pack of jackals—looking much like Anubis, Egyptian guardian of the dead—while working in the desert.

At about this time, British novelist Marie Corelli submitted a strange letter to the *New York World* magazine, warning of a mysterious punishment that could befall those who disturbed a sealed tomb. Other magazines and newspapers soon began publishing stories about a purported curse found inside the chambers of Tut's tomb.

Explorer Howard Carter (left) and his patron, Lord Carnarvon, are shown at the opening of King Tutankhamun's tomb in Egypt's Valley of the Kings in 1922. Carter's quest to find the tomb succeeded only after he convinced Carnarvon to support him for one last season.

Although Carter and his coworkers tried to dispel the rumor, the urban legend soon became accepted by millions of people. The myth only gained momentum on April 23, 1923, when Carnarvon died in Cairo's Continental-Savoy Hotel.

Carnarvon's Death Explained

Although most likely a result of blood poisoning from his mosquito bite that developed into pneumonia, daily newspaper reports seemed only to stoke belief in a curse. Arthur Conan Doyle, world-renowned author of the popular Sherlock Holmes mysteries, suggested that indeed Carnarvon's death could be attributed to an ancient curse created by Tutankhamun's priest during burial. Arthur Weigall, a respected former inspector-general of antiquities for the Egyptian government, appeared to echo the author's theory when he recalled that six weeks before his death, Carnarvon had entered the tomb laughing and joking about a curse.

During the first autopsy, or medical exam, of Tut's withered corpse, doctors found a healed blemish or lesion on the Pharaoh's left cheek, much like the one Carnarvon had gotten after cutting himself. Legend of the curse only proliferated when in 1925 Henry Field, an anthropologist, recalled meeting Carter and his friend Sir Bruce Ingham. Carter, reported Field, had given Ingham a desiccated, mummified hand to use as a paperweight on his desk. A bracelet around the wrist of the object had these words emblazoned on them: "Cursed be he who moves my body. To him shall come fire, water and pestilence."[11] According to Field, Ingham's house caught fire and burned to the ground. This tragedy was followed by a flood that washed the remains of the building away.

While such unexplained incidents seemed to swirl around those connected to the discovery of Tutankhamun's bejeweled tomb, a curse likely had little to do with it.

Of the 58 people present when the tomb was first entered in 1922, 8 died over the next 12 years, a statistically small number.

The curse aspect of the mummy legend would linger long into the twentieth century, but to uncover the true story of mummification and myth, it is necessary to turn back the clock and look for clues in the sweltering desert itself. There the secrets of the mummy's ageless appeal may truly lie.

Chapter 2

Separating Mummy from Myth

For archaeologists and anthropologists, mummies are fascinating artifacts of the ancient world. To these well-educated, rational scientists the mummy holds no supernatural power, and curses are little more than superstition. Yet for millions of others, mummy legends were once grounded in fact. The mummy, these believers suggested, stalked the night in order to avenge the corpse's unnatural disturbance. For Europeans in the nineteenth century, superstition remained alive and well. Despite scientific advancements, many maintained a belief in the supernatural. In Victorian England, the waning empire continued to be fascinated with the far-flung countries of the Middle East and North Africa, and decades of tomb plundering rendered the idea of the dead rising from their graves to be plausible. But to gain a fuller understanding of the mummy's appeal in the modern world, a closer look at the fertile region once populated and ruled by a great empire is necessary. There, kings and slaves raised great temples and carried out sacred rituals meant to help conquer the greatest earthly challenge of all: death.

Inhabitants of the Nile Valley

Contemporary fascination with mummies incorrectly suggests that Egyptian life was consumed with death. In reality, Egyptians lived complex and rich lives devoted to work and family. Greek historian Herodotus provided one of the earliest accounts of life in Egypt in the fifth century BC. There he found a land and a prosperous and happy people dependent upon the fertile soil created by yearly floods. He described the country as "the gift of the river."[12]

But Herodotus also observed many Egyptian religious practices. He became one of the first to describe the priests, whose shaven heads were unique among their kind in other regions he had visited. The depth of Egyptian belief was also noticed by the ancient historian, who said, "They are religious far beyond any other race of men."[13] An essential part of religious belief and worship involved sacred rituals concerning birth, life, and, finally, death. Yet Egyptians did not see death as a necessary end. Instead, they believed that thorough preparation of a corpse could ensure the departed person's entry into another world. Their mythology reinforced this dramatic and culture-altering idea. The central religious figure for early Egyptians was Osiris. Believed to be the first pharaoh, or king, he was, legend had it, wise and good. While Osiris left Egypt to share his infinite wisdom with the rest of the world, his beautiful wife, Isis, ruled the empire. Yet when Osiris returned, his conniving and jealous brother Set killed him, dismembered his body, and tossed it into the Nile. Set consequently seized the dead king's throne. Bereaved and brokenhearted, Isis eventually found the corpse and tied it back together, using strips of linen. With the help of Anubis, a jackal-headed god, Isis then restored life to her partner by literally breathing life back into him. Anubis embalmed Osiris, making him the first Egyptian mummy. Together briefly, Isis and Osiris conceived a son, the falcon-headed Horus. Although Osiris

> ## Did You Know?
>
> A recently identified mummy was revealed to be Hatshepsut, a female pharaoh who ruled from 1479 to 1458 BC.

could not return to the land of the living, he took his place in the afterlife and became the god of death, resurrection, and fertility. Anubis became the god of embalming.

A New Idea

Over time, the Egyptians realized that their dry and sand-filled part of the world was ideal for preserving the dead. While early mummies were created naturally by simply burying the deceased in the sand itself, as the generations passed, a precise and specific method of mummification evolved.

At some point, religious leaders began placing dead royalty in tombs with flat roofs. But these small structures did not prevent the

A wall painting from ancient Egypt depicts the ritualistic purification of the dead before entombment. The ancient Egyptians believed that preparation of the corpse would ensure its entry into the afterlife.

body's decay. The work to discover a way to keep the corpses intact continued. During the Third Dynasty, in 2630 BC, Pharaoh Djoser ordered that upon his death he be placed in an enormous and elaborate tomb. He called upon his capable adviser and respected high priest Imhotep to begin the design.

After much planning and forethought, Imhotep fashioned a steplike structure made from stone to house his great king. This would be the first pyramid. As the centuries passed, the Egyptians perfected mummification. By 1500 BC the process as it is known today had come into being.

The Art of Mummification

Mummification in ancient Egypt consisted of a series of painstakingly performed steps: First, the body was carefully washed and purified through prayer and ritual. Next, a priest cut a slit in the left side of the body with a sharp stone knife. The person who made the incision was ritualistically chased from the room as those around him threw rocks at him. This symbolized their disdain at the sacred body being violated. Then, workers or priests removed the lungs, liver, intestines, and stomach and embalmed them using natron—a white, salty substance found in nature that dried the organs out and prevented bacteria that caused decay from growing.

After drying, the organs were wrapped in linen and placed in four separate canopic jars, each depicting one of the god Horus's animal-headed sons. The heart was left in place, never to be removed. "The heart is kept in the mummification process because it is believed to be the soul of the person,"[14] says Sandra Olsen, curator of anthropology at the Carnegie Museum of Natural History. Once the organs were removed, the body cavity was stuffed with natron. The brain, apparently unappreciated by the Egyptians, was then pulled out piece by piece through the nose with a hook and typically thrown away. After this, the cadaver was placed on a slanted embalming table and doused with natron. The table's angle allowed any remaining bodily fluids to drain away from the body and encouraged the drying process. For at least 40 days, the deceased pharaoh lay drying until—slowly—the desiccated skin took on the appearance and toughness of leather. The

World's Oldest Mummies

Despite their claim on the contemporary imagination, Egyptian mummies were not the first mummies. Eight thousand years ago the Chinchorro people of coastal Peru placed their dead loved ones in the Atacama Desert, the driest place on Earth. There, the bodies were left flat on their backs; the sun's blazing heat did the rest. These "natural" mummies were eventually replaced by a process far more calculated and particular. Beginning in roughly 5000 BC, the Chinchorro took the deceased apart limb by limb and then reconnected the body using sticks, paste, and the elastic skin from sea lions.

With little direct knowledge of Chinchorro practices, cultures from other South and Central American countries such as Colombia, Ecuador, and Chile also began using mummification in their death rituals. The legendary Incas, who lived more than 500 years ago, mummified their dead from time to time—mainly children used in human sacrifices to appease their gods. But at times, adults were mummified too. One of the most famous of these is an Incan ruler whose name is lost to history. So precious and lifelike were his mummified remains that his people symbolically fed him and carried the mummy through the streets during religious rituals.

natron greatly aided this part of the process by speeding up the rate at which the body's liquid and moisture evaporated. Subsequently, the dried, hollowed-out body and head of the pharaoh were cleaned and then stuffed with sawdust, resin, linen, or a combination of all three. In this way, priests worked hard to re-create the shape and size of the departed. The slit on the left side of the body was then methodically sewn up and painted with an image of the protective eye of

Horus. Priests placed gold, jewels, and amulets—Egyptian good luck charms—upon the cadaver and then slowly and carefully wrapped it in 20 layers of soft linen strips. Resin—a gluey substance—was used to hold the pieces of linen together.

This ritualistic preparation was not only performed on humans. Over the generations, ancient Egyptians mummified millions of cats, dogs, and birds as well. This stemmed from a belief that particular gods found the animals to be sacred. Contrary to popular belief, great care was taken to preserve these creatures as well as if they had been human cadavers.

Funeral Rituals

The funeral ceremony itself, performed 70 days after the pharaoh's death, was solemn and dramatic. The mummy, snug inside its coffin, was placed on a bier and pulled by a team of oxen to the place of burial. A small band of musicians played a funeral dirge as they led the procession. Trailing behind them were the family of the dead and a coterie of priests, some of whom wore animal masks in imitation of the gods. The most important of these figures was the one dressed and masked as Anubis. Cartloads of splendid treasures and relics—many of them pure gold—followed. Ancient Egyptians believed that the dead could enjoy earthly pleasures in the afterlife and so they also brought food, wine, clothes, furniture, and even the bodies of loyal servants, many of whom were killed so that they could accompany their masters. Upon reaching the tomb, mourners proceeded inside for the sacred Opening of the Mouth ceremony. Performed by the Anubis-dressed priest,

> **Did You Know?**
>
> The ancient Egyptians are believed to have begun mummifying their dead as early as 2500 BC.

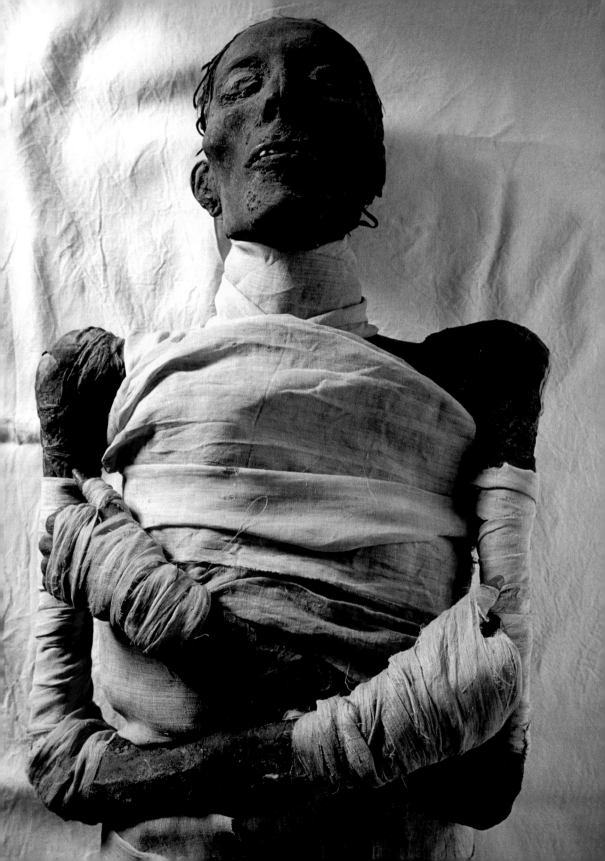

this ritual was believed to awaken or revive the senses of the dead person, thus allowing him to eat, drink, and speak in the afterlife. To begin, the Anubis imitator placed the coffin containing the mummy in a standing position facing south. Family members burned incense and draped freshly cut flowers near the head of the coffin; others painted a likeness of the deceased on it. Another high priest spoke religious incantations from the *Book of the Dead*, a volume of magic spells, and a newly slaughtered calf was provided as a blood sacrifice. A milk and salt purification rite was then performed, and finally, the Anubis-masked priest touched the mouth, eyes, ears, and nose of the dead with an adze, a sharp-bladed tool, to "wake" the person. At this, the coffin was placed in a large and ornate sarcophagus and sealed inside the dark tomb.

> **Did You Know?**
>
> Mummified human bodies, some naturally occurring and others created through religious rituals, have been found in locations as varied as South America, the Swiss Alps, Central Asia, and Alaska.

The Journey

Once ensconced in its tomb the journey into the afterlife began. Egyptians believed that the soul had two parts. One was the *ka*, a spirit version of the dead king's body that remained in the tomb with the dead and ate the food and drink that had been placed there. The ka could travel only within the confines of the burial chamber—from the body and into a statue or mold of the body. The other part, the *ba*, was the deceased person's character or personality.

In Egyptian imagery, the ba is often represented by a bird with a human head. The ba could roam freely into the wider world, but it had to return to the body from time to time, especially at night. In fact, traveling to the land of the dead was the ba's most essential and vital task. This is because each night Re, god of the sun, traveled through the Underworld on a return trip to become the sunrise. The ba followed Re and on the way encountered frightening and dangerous demons whose name the ba had to chant to defeat them. At the stroke of midnight the ba entered the Hall of Judgment, where it faced 42 Egyptian gods led by Osiris. Sitting before this array of gods, the ba had to utter a litany of confessions, after which the dead person's heart was placed on the Scale of Judgment. On the adjoining part of the scale were added two feathers, which were measured

Lady Dai: Mummy Mystery

Often referred to as the world's best-preserved ancient body, China's so-called Lady Dai has baffled scientists since she was discovered in 1971. That year, workers digging an air raid shelter in the town of Chansha in Hunan Province stumbled upon the tomb. Inside was the mummified corpse of a woman who had died more than 2,000 years ago, sometime between 178 and 145 BC. She died at about 50 years of age, according to DNA evidence, and was the wife of the Marquis of Han, a nobleman. Based on her corpulent appearance, researchers believe that her wealth and privilege provided her a rich diet, which likely contributed to her death from heart disease. She was buried wearing 20 layers of silk, and her tomb contains hundreds of items, including bamboo baskets of pears, plums, swans, pheasants, and pigs.

Most remarkable, though, is how intact the cadaver is. When it was found, the mummy's internal organs were in near perfect condition, as was her skin—soft to the touch— and still-bendable limbs. The blood still in her veins is type A. Scientists remain intrigued by the red liquid in which the body was submerged. Tests have revealed that this preservative contains a combination of magnesium and salt. "No one's found anything remotely equivalent to this," says anthropologist John Verano. "If she'd only been buried a year I would be amazed at how well-preserved she was."

Quoted in redOrbit, "Meet Lady Dai," November 4, 2004. www.redorbit.com.

against the sins of the heart. If the heart proved heavier than the feathers, it was picked up and given to Amut, a ferocious creature that combined parts of a hippopotamus, lion, and crocodile. Amut ate the heart and the person disappeared. If lighter than the feathers, the ba returned to the tomb and melded with the ka to become the *akh,* or immortal soul.

Warnings and Robbers

In Egypt's Old Kingdom, between 2686 and 2181 BC, this journey into the afterlife was considered so crucial that priests sometimes painted or carved warnings in tombs to deter anyone from disturbing them. The tomb of an ancient Egyptian governor, for example, contained this warning: "Any ruler who . . . shall do evil or wickedness to this coffin . . . may Hemen [a minor god] not accept any goods he offers, and may his heir not inherit." Another, from the tomb of a high-ranking official who lived around 2300 BC, said this: "As for all men who enter this my tomb . . . there will be judgment . . . an end shall be made for him. . . . I shall seize his neck like a bird . . . I shall cast the fear of myself into him."[15] Another warning invoked the anger of Thoth, the god of wisdom, and wished upon the interloper a disease-ridden death: "Cursed be those who disturb the rest of a Pharaoh. They that shall break the seal of this tomb shall meet death by a disease that no doctor can diagnose."[16]

> # Did You Know?
>
> Archaeologists working in Egypt have discovered the mummified remains of jackals, baboons, horses, and even a lion.

These rituals, beliefs, and warnings would, in future generations, provide vivid material for fiction writers and moviemakers as they tried to add an air of credibility and mystery to their fantastic and horrific tales of the macabre mummy. But at the time, superstition and stern admonitions were often trumped by the desire for the riches buried with the dead. Soon after pharaohs or the wealthy were encased in their tombs, robbers would plunder them, often escaping

Book of the Dead

One of the more intriguing surviving documents from ancient Egypt is the Book of the Dead. Written sometime before 1550 BC and used until approximately 50 BC, the volume contains a vast selection of magic spells. The purpose of these spells was to help guide the newly deceased through the underworld—known to Egyptians as the "Duat"—and into the afterlife. Part of a collection of other—often earlier—texts with similar purposes, including Pyramid Texts and Coffin Texts, the Book of the Dead was written in hieroglyphics on papyrus.

Wealthy families of the time often commissioned their own, personalized volumes, choosing particular spells that they thought might be most effective. The books were also colorfully illustrated to physically depict various journeys into the next world. So important was the information provided in the text that scenes from the work can also be found on existing tomb walls.

with priceless jewelry and gold. Royal tombs were of special interest to thieves because they likely contained the most valuable possessions. And the men who plundered the tombs had the best and easiest access to them: They were usually the tomb builders, who knew the secret passageways and false entries meant to discourage such thievery. Once inside, the bandits often lifted the lid of the sarcophagus, pried the coffin open, and quickly unwrapped the mummy to get at the jewels and amulets that had been placed in the linen folds. Believing the mummies themselves to be of little value, the tomb raiders typically burned them to heat their homes. Although these shady Egyptians were the first thieves to desecrate the tomb, they would not be the last. But they would leave it to others to worry about the warnings or curses that might follow their crimes.

Superstition and the Healing Power of Mummies

In AD 639, nearly seven centuries after Egypt's once glorious civilization had fallen to the Romans, the country became part of an Islam-controlled Arab empire. Before long, Egyptian beliefs melded with Muslim traditions. The Arabs were fascinated by but wary of the ancient Egyptians' beliefs. To them, Egyptian ways appeared strange and mysterious, particularly the hieroglyphics written on tomb walls and the Coptic language still spoken by some in the region. The Arab newcomers were intrgued by many aspects of Egyptian civilization, especially the belief that a particular mixture of potions and spells could transform the appearance of living matter.

Many Arabs believed in the power of magical words and that uttering them when entering a tomb could make visible the objects made invisible by the ancients. They superstitiously conceived of a power struggle in which the long-dead pharaohs and the contemporary Arabs of the period battled for possession of the fabulous golden treasures often buried deep in the desert sands. These early Arab inhabitants of the area also grew to believe that long-dead mummies could return to haunt, or even kill, the living. According to Egyptology scholar Christine El Mahdy, many drew this conclusion because of what they found inside the burial chambers. "The belief that mummies could be restored to life grew from the paintings on the walls of ancient tombs. . . . The idea that the dead could move, see, smell, hear, taste and touch made the mummy a powerful adversary—more threatening than a living enemy since this one was already dead and had nothing to fear."[17]

Later, in the twelfth century, a western translator mistakenly confused a reference to a type of bitumen—a sticky tar-like substance—listed in an Arabic medical book with the type the ancient Egyptians used to wrap their mummies. The mistake was easy to make since Persians referred to it as "mumiya." The mistake started a belief that mummies had some sort of healing power. Before long, Europeans were seeking mummies for medicinal purposes. Once purchased, the ancient cadavers were ground into powder and placed into drinks and elixirs to cure headaches, backaches, and a host of other ailments.

This continued for centuries—from the Middle Ages into the Renaissance and beyond. Such was the hunger for mummy-based powders, the mummy itself mattered little. "To satisfy this almost insatiable demand for mummies in the West, the production of hundreds of fake mummies became commonplace," writes Egyptologist Werner Seipel. "One did not even shy away from mummifying the bodies of newly deceased persons and turning them into mummy-medicine."[18]

This new market for mummies was a boon for thieves who were previously only interested in the tomb's golden treasures. The wealthiest and most powerful people of Europe convinced themselves that mummy medicines kept them fit and feeling good. "Europe's wealthy intelligentsia swore by the drug," says historian Heather Pringle. "The French king Francis I, a patron of Leonardo Da Vinci and the very soul of an enlightened monarch, wore a small packet of mummy and powdered rhubarb around his neck to remedy an emergency."[19]

The spirit of the deceased travels into the afterlife in this Egyptian wall painting from about 1306 to 1290 BC. Many such paintings have been found in tombs along with jewels and everyday items intended to make the afterlife more pleasurable.

European Conquest of Egypt

French emperor Napoléon's sojourn in Egypt in 1798 further ushered in a wave of interest in all things Egyptian. It was Europe's first direct contact with the great civilization since ancient times. During that trip, Napoléon brought with him a broad bevy of scientists and scholars to study the country. One result of their studies was a massive, 24-volume look at the Nile nation—its culture, its people, and its beliefs. Published between 1808 and 1829, it formed the basis of a scientific discipline soon to be known as Egyptology. Later, pressed by France and Great Britain's desire for access to Egypt's antiquities, the nation's ruler, Mohammed Ali, agreed. The two European rivals set about finding and retrieving the greatest number of artifacts. For decades, wealthy European tourists poured into Cairo, Luxor, and the surrounding areas to ride camels in the shadows of the great pyramids. Most of these tourists cared little about the fragile nature of the sandy treasures. Tomb robbers took their share of objects, too, often smuggling dozens of mummies out of the country and selling them to traveling sideshows and carnivals on the American and European black markets. Misuse of these precious artifacts was notorious and widespread.

Did You Know?

In the nineteenth century, countless mummies were burned as firewood in areas of Egypt where trees were scarce.

According to historian Jasmine Day, contemporary views of the mummy as a monster stem from two separate but related nineteenth-century legends. The first is the creepy but romantic idea of love between a mortal and a once-dead mummy that comes back to life. The other is the notion of a mummy's curse placed upon future tomb robbers by ancient, long-dead Egyptian priests. Throughout the nineteenth century, scholars and treasure hunters took what they could from hundreds if not thousands of tombs. By 1900 stricter controls over archaeological digs were put in place, but by then it was often too late.

Wealthy Europeans of the nineteenth century paid handsome sums to import newly found mummies. Shiploads of bandaged carcasses traveled west, and once they arrived, they were often unwrapped and boiled. The resulting oil was sold in stores as a way of treating bruises and other common ailments. In the United States, Americans took the linen wrapping material and converted it into paper products. The pervasive use of mummy parts became a fad among many, with chic couples throwing mummy parties. During such soirees, the main event of the night included guests taking turns uncovering the mummies themselves. As a consequence, the mummies were destroyed, their historical value lost forever. In most cases the precious artifacts had been smuggled out of Egypt illegally.

The demand for mummies increased. This encouraged tomb robbing on a larger scale than ever before. The attraction for thieves was obvious: Not only could they sell the mummies to a fevered Western clientele, but the jewels, amulets, and other precious items could also earn a high price. The illegal nature of the enterprise ensured that any record of the mummy having ever been discovered was lost. By the time of Howard Carter's famous discovery, it is no wonder that so many experts had doubted that King Tut's tomb would ever reveal itself. To most people in Europe and the United States in the late nineteenth and early twentieth centuries, mummies were no more frightening than their own family's cemetery plots. But that would soon change, prompted by continued British occupation and control over Egyptian politics and culture. As English archaeologists unearthed relics of Egypt's glorious past, many Egyptians came to believe that their history was being stolen by colonial interlopers. This Egyptian belief that their past had been unjustly taken from them may have prompted the rumors of ancient curses that soon followed and would, in time, form the basis of much of today's mummy mania.

Chapter 3

Mummy Legends and Curses

Much of the mummy's power derives not from actual murders or mayhem. Instead it comes from the myths and legends that have sprouted up over the millennia. At times, the imagination conquers reason and shatters certainty, even among those least likely to believe in the supernatural. When King Tut's tomb was first discovered, most people had never heard of the "Curse of the Pharaohs." Fewer still were aware that some of the earliest Egyptian tombs contained stern warnings against disturbing the sacred dead. While most legitimate scientists and scholars scoff at the notion of curses, weird and hard-to-explain events sometimes conspire to make the heartiest skeptics look over their shoulders during a dig or to walk a little faster when leaving a tomb. Thus, although science can often root out the obvious hoaxes, other mummy stories appear to defy any sort of logical explanation.

"Curse of the Pharaohs" Continued?

The "Curse of the Pharaohs" did not end with Carter's amazing discovery in 1922. Although no curse was found written on King Tut's tomb or inside his burial chamber, journalists and experts of the time often perpetuated the idea of one to sell newspapers or make names for themselves. One of these, an English Egyptologist named Arthur Weigall, was respected in his field. Thus, his two curse-related stories made any doubters reluctant to come forward. Weigall had worked for years in the Valley of the Kings and had made a number of tomb discoveries, yet Carter's glorious find overshadowed Weigall's accomplishments and those of other archaeologists in the region.

Weigall, though, would not be silent. He published a book of his thoughts and recollections called *Tutankhamen and Other Essays* in 1924. In it he describes a number of incidents that only reinforce the notion of mummy-related supernatural happenings. In one, he chronicles the death of Howard Carter's snake-bitten pet canary. In another, Weigall describes one priceless artifact that he had purchased: a cat-shaped, wooden sarcophagus that had once contained the mummified remains of a long-dead cat. He had, he claims, left it next to him when he went to sleep one night. His deep and dreamless slumber was suddenly shattered by a sound like a loud gunshot. Opening his eyes, Weigall was greeted by a large gray cat; on the floor laid the splintered and broken cat coffin. The cat departed, leaving the groggy archaeologist stricken with fear.

> ## Did You Know?
> Egyptologist Arthur Weigall was infuriated by Lord Carnarvon's exclusive business deals that allowed only him to profit from the discovery of King Tut's tomb.

A stranger and more dangerous event recounted by Weigall concerns him and his friend, American artist Joseph Lindon Smith, and their wives. Intoxicated by the beauty and mystery of Egypt's Valley of the Queens, the four devised to put on an outdoor play there. But during a rehearsal, Smith's wife, Corinna, felt a stabbing pain in her eyes. Later, Weigall's wife, Hortense, felt stabbing pains in her stomach. The rehearsal had to be stopped; the ailing women were rushed to the hospital. Struck by an acute sense of foreboding, the men quickly canceled the play's scheduled performances. Weigall actively promoted the curse idea, but nearly a century later it is clear that logical explanations can be found for his so-called mysterious occurrences. The cracked cat coffin likely warped and broke in the humid Egyptian night. This probably caused the cat that appeared on his bed to be spooked. Corinna Smith's eye pain, it has now been determined, was inevitably the result of an acute eye condition caused by hours spent in the hot sun without sunglasses. Finally, Hortense Weigall's abdominal discomfort was due to the fact that she was pregnant with Arthur Weigall's child during their sojourn to the desert. There is no report of the couple's child in any way being affected by the infamous curse, yet two other children may have haunted a contemporary Egyptologist and driven him to take extreme measures.

Child Mummies' Curse

In 1999 Zahi Hawass, Egypt's undersecretary of state for Giza monuments, and a team of researchers discovered something extraordinary. A few years before, near the city of El Bawiti in Egypt's western desert, a farmer's donkey had stumbled upon a deep but narrow hole in the sand. This accidental misstep would prove to be a historical gold mine in which 60 gilded mummies, painted chests, and detailed masks were found by Hawass and his crew of archaeologists. Showing few, if any, signs of looting, this Valley of the Golden Mummies revealed glorious treasures from the first and second centuries AD, when Egyptians lived under Roman occupation. The up to 10,000 people buried there, it was soon determined, were likely not of royal lineage but were instead wealthy merchants, whose affluence bought them greater hope for peace and prosperity in the afterlife. In June 1999 Hawass made the official announcement of the find, which brought reporters from around the world. Pressured by travel agents and the Egyptian government to open these tombs to the public, Hawass initially balked. But after further persuasion, he agreed to allow the government to showcase five of the mummies at the nearby Bahariya Museum. Two of them, he decided, would be the mummies of children. It was at this moment, Hawass said, that he remembered the infamous "Curse of the Pharaohs" surrounding the discovery of Tut's tomb in 1922. Although his rational self found such legends clichéd and silly, his own work had brought with it a series of strange coincidences. During his first dig, for example, he had removed a load of precious gold objects from a cemetery to the Egyptian Museum in Cairo. Tragedy had followed: "That same day, my cousin died," he

> ## Did You Know?
>
> In 1999 a microbiologist identified potentially dangerous mummy mold spores that are unleashed when a long-buried body is uncovered. Illness, he suggested, could follow and promote the idea of a mummy's curse.

said. "Two years later, on the anniversary of that day, my uncle died. On the same day of the third year, my aunt died."[20]

The Nightmares Begin

Although he had noticed the odd pattern, Hawass had tried to ignore the possibility of any connection to a curse. Yet the concept of mummy curses continued to bother him. Later, during the excavation of a previously undisturbed crypt at the Tombs of the Pyramid Builders at Giza, he was confronted by a provocative message written inside: "O all people who enter this tomb, who will make evil against this tomb and destroy it, may the crocodile be against them on water and snakes against them on land. May the hippopotamus be against them on water, the scorpion against them on land."[21]

Now, as Hawass and two helpers prepared the mummies of two long-dead children—a brother and sister—for transport to the museum, he became haunted by the curse idea. During the two-hour process, he pondered the supernatural, his reluctance to move the bodies from their resting place, and his own experience with strange, mummy-related occurrences.

That night, after a severe bout of insomnia, Hawass drifted into a nightmare in which the two children—whose faces he knew all too well from his work—followed him through a house. Wherever he turned and no matter how much he tried to escape them, he could not. They clutched at him with outstretched arms; he was terrified. And then he came upon an adult female mummy, known to him and his team as Mummy B. Although she smiled at him in his dream, her eyes pleaded with him. What did she want from him, he wondered? He could not tell.

Resting in Peace

Hawass moved to Los Angeles, California, in the late 1990s to teach for the summer at UCLA. There, he continued to dream of the mummy siblings. As his archaeological fame grew in the United States, so too did the frequency of his nightmares. It seemed that the more national exposure he received on American television and in

Mummified Monks of Japan

One of the more unusual mummy-related practices was popular among Buddhist monks in Japan in the nineteenth and early twentieth centuries. Known as self-mummification, nirvana-seeking men went through a three-step process to become *sokushinbutsu*, or "living mummies." First, for 1,000 days the monks would eat nothing but nuts and seeds and engage in strenuous physical exercise meant to cleanse the body of fat. Next, they would switch their diet to one consisting of plant roots and tree bark. As their bodies grew thinner, they began drinking a special toxic tea made from the sap of the urushi tree and water containing the poison arsenic. Gradually, this would drain the body of moisture. During the final step of the process, the monks entered a cramped, underground room connected to the surface by only a long bamboo air pipe through which they would breathe. The monks would remain inside meditating, with no further food or drink, until they died. After this, fellow monks sealed the chamber, which had now become a tomb. After another 1,000 days, fellow monks would enter the dead men's space and wash them. The best-preserved were known as living mummies. These macabre attempts at self-mummification were typically unsuccessful, but the mummies that do exist provide a haunting example of self-sacrifice.

newspapers, the more persistent his nocturnal torture became. Then one night, as the little girl mummy again reached out to clutch Hawass's throat, he woke up screaming. He had agreed to appear at the Richmond Art Museum in Virginia that night and had to rise for an early flight. But the promised taxicab never came. The delay meant that he did not arrive in Richmond until 7:30 p.m. He rushed to the museum but did not begin his lecture until 9:00. His talk that night concerned the curse of the mummies, but he kept his own recent nightmares and the children that haunted him to himself.

During a late dinner with the museum director and her husband, the woman reminded Hawass of his promised lecture the following morning to a group of teachers. Again, as on so many other nights, he had a hard time sleeping; he feared who might visit him. Hawass eventually fell into a fitful slumber but awoke a few hours later to the sound of loud knocking on his door from the hotel staff; he had overslept and missed the lecture.

Later in the day, as he arrived at the Richmond airport for his flight back to Los Angeles, he decided to give deeper thought to the mummy siblings and the day they had been moved. Then, as he prepared to board the plane the solution came to him: "I know why the children are upset," Hawass said to himself. "They need to have their father with them."[22] When he returned to Egypt that fall, he ordered the father's mummy moved to Bahariya Museum. From that day forward, the mummy children never returned to Hawass's

An extraordinary find in Egypt's western desert took place in the 1990s when a farmer and his donkey stumbled upon a deep hole. Within the hole lay painted chests, masks, and 60 gilded mummies (pictured). The site, later named the Valley of the Golden Mummies, showed few signs of looting.

dreams. Although he remains skeptical about curses, he believes that mummies should not be displayed. Instead, they should remain in their burial chambers, just as they were found.

The Unlucky Mummy

Hawass's belief that museums should not display the mummified remains of ancient people is no doubt supported by the legend of the Unlucky Mummy. Strangely, the curse was tied not to a mummy at all but to its inner coffin lid. Measuring 64 inches (162 cm) in length and hand-painted a chalky white, the wooden and plaster board was unearthed at Thebes in the mid-1800s. Modern archaeologists have dated the object to the late 21st or early 22nd Egyptian dynasty, or roughly 950–900 BC. Painted on this lid is a beardless face, which indicates that the coffin contained the body of a mummified woman. Although the wood does have short religious inscriptions written on it in hieroglyphics, no other identification exists. Scientists have surmised that because of the lid's high quality and ornate etchings, the woman must have been a high priestess or of royal blood.

The alleged facts of the "mummy" are that it was first purchased in Luxor, Egypt, by a group of four British travelers in the 1890s. To sweeten the purchase, the seller told the wealthy young men that the case had contained the remains of the princess of Amen-Ra, a mysterious 4,000-year-old royal. The friends drew lots, and the man who won gladly paid the thousands of pounds being asked for the piece. After having the coffin hauled to his hotel, the man wandered through the streets of the city and out into the desert, never to be seen again.

On the following day, one of the three remaining Englishmen was shot accidently by his Egyptian servant. Although he survived, his injured arm was soon amputated. The last two men soon after suffered from financial ruin and debilitating illness. Wherever the "mummy" was housed, doom followed—from fires to hauntings. Madame Blavatsky, a noted spiritualist of the early twentieth century, publically condemned the artifact as evil. The object changed hands a number of times before being donated to the British Museum by a collector named A.F. Wheeler. Legend has it that as the piece was unloaded from a truck the vehicle suddenly went into reverse and pinned a bystander. Later, as a pair of workmen carried it up the stairs to its display case, one of the men tripped, fell, and broke his leg. Two days later, the other workman died under mysterious circumstances.

Mysterious Deaths

The coffin's reputation for bad luck did not diminish with age. Evening security guards reported hearing sounds of a hammer—as if someone were trying to escape—and mournful weeping and sobbing. After a night of unrest, other exhibits were found to have been moved, even violently thrown around the room during the night. Before long, workers refused to enter the same room as the coffin; one may have died. In one hard-to-verify case, a child contracted measles and died after a blasé visitor tossed his handkerchief at the face painted on the relic.

> # Did You Know?
>
> In the 1970s a police officer guarding a King Tut funerary mask suffered a stroke; he later blamed it on the infamous curse.

At that point, museum curators agreed to move the coffin to the basement. But even there it wreaked havoc when an archivist became sick and a supervisor died at this post. Terrified, the museum desperately sought a buyer for the ancient heirloom, but there were no takers until, in 1912, an American archaeologist purchased the piece and arranged for it to be shipped to the United States. It was boxed up and carried aboard an ocean liner. This ship, the *Titanic*, never reached its destination. It sank in the North Atlantic on April 15, 1912. In all, 1,517 passengers and crew perished. The coffin, too, the story suggests, sank to the bottom of the ocean.

Yet while this widely circulated legend remains of interest to mummy fanatics around the world, the truth is far more mundane. This coffin lid of death can be seen in the British Museum today. It did not sink with the *Titanic*. The legend of the "Unlucky Mummy" itself was the invention of two British journalists, William Stead and Douglas Murray. But what began in their imaginations as pure fiction was eventually blended with the face-painted coffin that the two men saw during a visit to the British Museum. Soon after, they sold their bizarre story of a mummy's curse to London newspapers.

A Logical Explanation

Jasmine Day also sees in the legend of the Unlucky Mummy a transatlantic rivalry between the United States and Great Britain. Depending on which version of the story is told, many of its details are either connected to Great Britain or the United States. The supernatural aspects, she suggests, were added by enterprising journalists and spiritualists. Day also believes that the curse idea as it relates to the Unlucky Mummy was based in large part on the attitudes of people at the turn of the century.

In particular, many believed that Egypt had been terribly abused and stolen from as a colony of the British Empire. Some, therefore, feared retribution for this theft. "Like the curse fiction that preceded it, the Unlucky Mummy myth interwove two prevailing attitudes," writes Day, "Egypt as wronged avenger and Egypt as infernal menace."[23] This Western fear of what the archaeological expeditions and abuse of ancient artifacts might have brought only further promoted the idea of mummy-connected curses.

Regardless of the tale's origin, its hold on skeptics and believers alike is hard to shake.

According to early twentieth-century Egyptologist and anthropologist Margaret Alice Murray, university fields trips to the museum often prompted strange responses in her students: "I used to take my students to the British Museum. . . . I always had to stop . . . and say . . . 'We are now going into the room where the so-called Unlucky Mummy is; if you believe in it you needn't come. . . .' To my surprise, I found always there were a certain number of people who wouldn't face the thing."[24]

Mummy of Bessemer Hall

Another mummy that has struck fear into those who viewed it was that of Hazel Farris, born in Bessemer, Alabama, in 1880. Farris grew to be a true southern belle in post–Civil War America but was also known for her feisty spirit. Never one to abide by her generation's rules of female propriety, Farris could take care of herself. She had to. Her relationships with men were typically marked by violence. By her mid-twenties, she was living in Kentucky with a hard-drinking husband, and neighbors often complained to authorities about the yelling coming from the household.

On August 6, 1905, Hazel and her husband—whose name history does not record—got into a drunken brawl. Dishes, furniture, and fists began to fly. Hazel gave as good as she got, and then some. She found the man's pistol and pumped three bullets into his body. The neighbors alerted police, but when three officers entered the house, they too were killed by Hazel's smoking gun. A deputy sheriff arrived soon after, and at first it looked as if he could restrain her. In their ensuing gun battle, he shot off one of her fingers. But Hazel would not go quietly; he shook off her injury and murdered the deputy, too. She then escaped and returned to her hometown of Bessemer.

Despite a warrant for her arrest and a $500 reward for her capture, Hazel somehow eluded authorities. She may have changed her name or her appearance, but she somehow found a way to resume a normal life. She found a job, perhaps in a general store or as a housekeeper, and eventually fell in love. In some versions of this urban legend, the man was a police officer. Their passionate relationship was destroyed, though, when in a moment of passion she confessed her crimes to her lover. Whether the man was horrified by her past crimes or simply wanted the hefty reward, he soon after told authorities that Hazel was a murderess. Distraught and heartbroken, Hazel drank a lethal mixture of arsenic and gasoline on December 20, 1906. By the time police arrived on the scene, she was dead.

Renowned Egyptian archaeologist Zahi Hawass (pictured at the entrance of a painted rock-hewn tomb) had nightmares about two child mummies that had been separated from the mummy of their father. Once the three were reunited, the nightmares stopped.

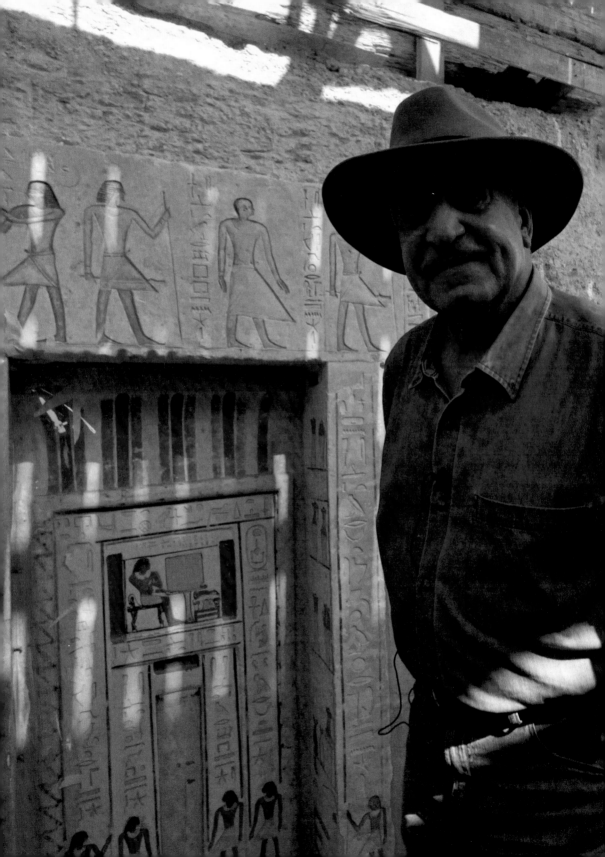

Hazel's body was moved to Adams Vermillion, a local furniture store that doubled as a funeral parlor. Because no family members claimed her corpse, Mr. Adams decided to put her in storage until he could decide what to do. Strangely, over the next few months Hazel's body showed no signs of decay. In fact, her cadaver had started to mummify. Perhaps, Adams thought, it was the unique combination of arsenic—a poison—and the gasoline that had somehow acted as a preservative. Being the entrepreneur he was, Adams began charging 10 cents to view Hazel's mummified remains.

On Display

When Bessemer crowds began to thin, Adams loaned the body to his brother in Tuscaloosa and military man Harvey Lee Boswell. Eventually, Adams sold the ghoulish treasure to entrepreneur O.C. Brooks, who featured it in a traveling sideshow for nearly 40 years. At his retirement, Brooks left the human relic to his nephew with the stipulation that profits raised from its exhibition now had to be given entirely to charity. Although records are sketchy, legend has it that some of the proceeds went toward building dozens of churches in Tennessee.

Finally, from 1974 to 2004 the mummy of Hazel Farris was on display in her hometown at the Bessemer Hall of History. Superstitious patrons and workers reported lights switching on and off and occasional eerie and unexplainable whistling noises. Although Hazel was finally buried in 2005, many believe her ghost still haunts the museum. Skeptics, on the other hand have poked holes in a number of aspects of the story. No records from the state of Kentucky exist to verify the death of four police officers on August 6, 1905. A National Geographic documentary produced about Hazel's mummy includes an autopsy of the desiccated corpse. Although examiners verified that the missing finger was

Did You Know?

Ancient Egyptians believed that their souls were kept alive when their names were remembered.

John Wilkes Booth: The Mummy

John Wilkes Booth, assassin of Abraham Lincoln, 16th president of the United States, was shot and killed in a Virginia barn on April 26, 1865. At least that is what most history books on the subject would have you believe. But one conspiracy theory posits that Booth escaped and that the American government covered it up. Lincoln's murderer, meanwhile, made his way to South America. Then on January 13, 1903, a man named David E. George died in Enid, Oklahoma. Before he did he confessed to his landlady, Mrs. Harper, that he was Booth.

What began as a deathbed revelation quickly became the talk of the town. In late January the rumor made the local newspaper. Enid officials had the body embalmed but refused it burial until the speculation could be put to rest, but that never happened. The body was subsequently mummified and displayed at the undertaker's parlor until purchased by Memphis lawyer Fenis L. Bates, who joined a circus sideshow in the early 1900s and toured the country with the reputed mummy of Booth's corpse.

Like the curse legends that circulated in the aftermath of the King Tut discovery, hard-to-verify stories about the mummy's lethal effects soon passed from town to town. In some versions sideshow owners met with financial disaster, and a train on which the mummy was traveling crashed and killed eight people. Bates sold few people on the Booth mummy story; he died broken and penniless in 1923. While most legitimate historians scoff at the notion that David E. George was really John Wilkes Booth, the urban legend remains one of the stranger chapters in mummy history.

likely shot off a year before Hazel's death, they determined she died of pneumonia, not poisoning.

Yet adding to the mystery is the fact that the body is full of arsenic, but investigators determined that she had not ingested it; instead, she was pickled in it. Since Bessemer had no certified embalmers at the time, those who prepared her dead body may have simply submerged her in the arsenic as a primitive but effective way of embalming her. One conclusion drawn by the National Geographic investigators is that many of the events surrounding the life and death of Hazel Farris went unrecorded, suggesting that the legend itself may have been contrived by the exhibitors of her mummy.

"Since Hazel was a sideshow mummy, to make her story better they embellished her past," said Jerry Conlogue from the National Geographic team. "We wanted to find what was true about Hazel's past. Because we did an autopsy on Hazel, we were able to answer a few mysteries."[25]

Mummy legends remain intriguing but difficult-to-verify phenomena. Scientists willing to take a closer look at the ongoing mysteries surrounding mummies and myth often find that once-accepted fact crumbles under the weight of close, rational examination. But although mummy legends are usually revealed as hoaxes or harmless invention, the stranglehold that those cloddish creatures have over popular culture remains stronger than ever.

Chapter 4

The Mummy and Popular Culture

Nowhere has the mummy as monster idea been more toyed with, more twisted, than in contemporary popular culture. While movies may provide the most effective and lingering portrait of the raggedy, homicidal linen-wearer, other artistic expressions have added depth and staying power to the mummy. In comics, cartoons, comedies, and in literature, this cultural icon has fired the imaginations of many of the world's most creative people. The mummy as muse simply will not die.

Mummies in Literature

American writer and humorist Mark Twain's muse was the Mississippi River; in books such as *The Adventures of Tom Sawyer* and *Huckleberry Finn*, the former Samuel Clemens painted a complex portrait of life along the mighty river's muddy banks. In 1869 Twain chronicled his travels in a popular book called *The Innocents Abroad*. During a stop in Egypt, Twain noticed that ancient mummies were no more precious to Egyptians than they were to Europeans in the nineteenth century.

With his trademark wit and sly use of irony, Twain describes a scene he witnessed: "Egyptian railroad engineers fueled their locomotives with discarded mummies from local tombs and graveyards. Stacked like so much fire wood, the mummies were simply shoveled into the train's boilers when called for. One engineer joked to another to stop using the dried corpses of common people. 'They don't burn worth a cent,' he said. 'Pass out a king!'"[26]

Nearly 40 years earlier, one of the first modern mummy novels was written by British-born Jane Webb Loudon. Loudon, born in 1807, was raised in wealth, but her father soon lost the family fortune. Left penniless, Loudon determined to support her family through her pen. In fact, while going through her papers, she realized she might already have a literary product to sell. "I had written a strange, wild novel, called the Mummy," she later said, "in which I had laid the scene in the twenty-second century, and attempted to predict the state of improvement to which this country might possibly arrive."[27] This novel, *The Mummy! A Tale of the Twenty-Second Century*, was published anonymously in 1827. Set in the year 2126 in England, the story concerns a corrupt government restored to honor by a scientifically revived Egyptian mummy.

The novel may have been inspired by France's conquest of Egypt as well as a public mummy party in London's Piccadilly Circus that Loudon attended as a young girl. Whatever the initial inspiration, the popularity and power of *Frankenstein*, written by Mary Shelley and published in 1818 may have offered Loudon the encouragement she needed. Still, she published her mummy novel anonymously, fearing criticism by the mostly male critics of the day. To her delight, many critics loved the book and its many strange and intriguing scientific inventions, including an information highway not unlike today's Internet.

Did You Know?

In "Ligeia," Edgar Allan Poe's 1838 story, a man has his wife wrapped in bandages in preparation for burial.

Stoker's Jewel

Loudon's contribution to mummy literature is little remembered today by most readers, but the literary services of Irish author Bram Stoker are hard to forget. Stoker gained literary immortality for the gothic vampire novel *Dracula* in 1897. Six years later Stoker spooked readers again with *The Jewel of Seven Stars*.

The story begins with a mystery. A young lawyer named Malcolm Ross is summoned in the middle of the night to the home of Margaret Trelawney. When he arrives, Malcolm discovers Margaret in the company of a policeman and a doctor. The three of them are frightened by a mysterious attack made on Margaret's father, an eminent archaeologist. Slashed in the left arm and bleeding, the man is

Like all good movie mummies, the mummy in the 1944 film The Mummy's Curse (*pictured*) *emerges from its tomb wrapped in soiled, rotting strips of linen and carries out its evil deeds. Mummies have also found their way into other areas of popular culture, including books and cartoons.*

found on the floor of his room. Much like in *Dracula*, careful watch is given the victim, but he is still attacked a second time. Eventually, Malcolm and Margaret deduce that the powerful intruder desires to open the safe located in the injured man's room. The house, it turns out, is filled with Egyptian relics.

Before long the tale of crime takes on supernatural overtones. After recovering, Professor Trelawney tells his daughter and her friend that he has been attacked by a risen mummy, Queen Tera. Her bandaged cadaver is kept as a souvenir in the professor's study. The ailing academic suggests that the queen's time for rebirth has come: "She, who was guided by augury, and magic, and superstition, naturally chose a time for her resurrection which seemed to have been pointed out by the High Gods themselves."[28] But to complete the process Queen Tera will require the jewel of seven stars, which is kept in the professor's safe.

The book's darker ending met with criticism from readers and critics alike. Before publishing a new edition of the novel in 1912, editors convinced the author to modify the ending to make it happier. But not until Penguin Books re-released *The Jewel of Seven Stars* in 2008 was Stoker's original conclusion restored.

> ## Did You Know?
>
> *Little Women* author Louisa May Alcott wrote a story in 1869 called "Lost in a Pyramid." In it she features one of the first uses of a mummy's curse to drive the plot.

Mummy Meets Movies

The twentieth century also brought with it the new technologies of flight, automobiles, and the cinema. Yet the ongoing popularity of the mummy suggested that the public still yearned for the ancient world and longed to know its secrets. With the advent of the motion picture, novels and plays were appropriated for portrayal on the big screen. The earliest known mummy movie was a 1911 film called *The Mummy* in which a female mummy is brought to life and causes problems for a young scientist and his love interest.

A Traveling Exhibition

Acontinued interest in preserved bodies and body parts may explain the enormous popularity of a traveling exhibition known as *Body Worlds*. The brainchild of German anatomist Gunter von Hagens, the show features real human specimens that have been put through a process known as plastination. The result is a unique, if ghoulish, skinless cadaver in which a viewer can clearly see the muscles, tendons, organs, and other internal structures of the body. First shown in Tokyo, Japan, in 1995, *Body Worlds* has since toured more than 50 museums around the world to mixed reviews. It includes 25 full-body plastinates and more than 200 organs. One of the more popular exhibits features a scarred liver and blackened lungs of a heavy smoker set next to the liver and lungs of a nonsmoker. To complete the desired effect, Hagens employs more than 300 technicians in 5 laboratories in Germany, China, and Kyrgyzstan.

While the exhibit's promotional literature touts its mission as educational, critics have argued that Hagens is exploiting—perhaps abusing—the human form with his displays of neatly sliced and arranged livers, torsos, and faces. Although Hagens claims that all specimens are taken from people who freely donated their bodies, critics claim that he buys cadavers wherever he can find them. Some Christian and Jewish groups have also objected to *Body Worlds*, believing that it defiles the sanctity of the human form. Despite the controversies, millions of people each year flock to this strange new form of mummification.

Two decades later came Karloff's 1932 movie of the same name; it provided Hollywood producers the opportunity to revive the formula over and over again in the coming years. Soon, the mummy genre became a bankable B-movie staple that audiences—and cash-hungry movie executives—could count on. By definition, these films were cheaply made, included second-tier stars, and were given relatively little promotion by movie studios.

One of the first post-Karloff mummy pictures starred Lon Chaney Jr., a character actor whose father, Lon Chaney, had been known as the "Man of a Thousand Faces." Like him, Chaney Jr. played a wide variety of roles, but in 1941 he headlined the Universal horror flick *The Wolf Man.* Chaney Jr., transforming from average Joe to hairy terror baying at the moon, was so convincing to audiences that the actor was soon typecast. Although the work kept coming, he would forever be identified with the role. Yet in 1942 Chaney Jr. starred in *The Mummy's Tomb.* In the picture, the actor played Kharis, a mystery man sent by an Egyptian high priest to avenge the desecration of the tomb of Princess Ananka. In time, Chaney Jr. would earn the distinction of playing the complete quartet of classic screen monsters: Dracula's son, Frankenstein's monster, the wolf man, and the mummy. He returned as the linen-clad killer in 1944's *The Mummy's Ghost.* Again, Chaney Jr. played Kharis, this time kidnapping a beautiful young woman that he suspects is the reincarnated princess.

A spate of similar movies followed, some better and some quite terrible. In 1959 charismatic Christopher Lee played the role of the mummy in another movie of the same name for Britain's Hammer Film Productions. The story centers on archaeologist John Banning, who hits the relic jackpot when he discovers a hidden tomb. Yet his riches come at a price: Banning's father goes mad, and death haunts a number of the scientist's colleagues. Lee, the star of the show, plays a former high priest and now guardian of the tomb. Sent by a disciple of the Egyptian god Osiris to avenge the opening of the tomb, Lee's mummy towers over his victims and strangles them. According to one critic, the movie is best remembered for its chilling yet unseen tongue removing scene.

Lee's physical performance, in which he dramatically crashes through windows and doors to throttle those foolish enough to disturb his sacred tomb, terrified audiences. His success as the mummy led to his casting in his signature role as Count Dracula during the 1960s in a series of creepy and unique vampire flicks for Hammer.

NAMELESS!
FLESHLESS!
DEATHLESS!

The MUMMY'S GHOST

starring
LON CHANEY
as Kharis, The Mummy
with
JOHN CARRADINE
RAMSAY AMES
BARTON MacLANE
GEORGE ZUCCO
ROBERT LOWERY

Good and Bad

Apart from the Hammer Films version, by the late 1950s the image of the moaning mummy often seemed more silly than scary. Comedy duo Bud Abbott and Lou Costello played it for laughs in their 1955 movie *Abbott and Costello Meet the Mummy*. The two played witless Americans looking for work. They meet up with an Egyptologist and before long are in the middle of murders, mummies, and mayhem. Years earlier another comedy team, the Three Stooges, starred in *We Want Our Mummy*. That 1939 short remains one of the classics of the genre, as Moe, Larry, and Curly are trapped in a tomb and come face to face with the mummy of long-dead pharaoh Rootin' Tootin'.

But while both of those movies intended a humorous take on ancient Egypt, others were unintentionally funny. One less than

Actor Lon Chaney Jr. had the distinction of playing the classic quartet of movie monsters: Dracula's son, Frankenstein's monster, the wolf man, and the mummy. He acted the part of the mummy several times, including in the 1944 film The Mummy's Ghost.

memorable screen incarnation, *The Curse of the Mummy's Tomb* from 1964, features a mummy named Ra-Antef. The story was by then familiar and included dark and deadly curses and piles of innocent victims. That same year brought *Wrestling Women vs. the Aztec Mummy*. Featuring the titled showdown between a group of masked Mexican wrestlers and a South American mummy named Xochitl, the movie also includes an Asian gang fronted by tough guy Black Dragon. In this feature the mummy also has the power to transform itself into a snake or bat. Often compared with the 1959 film *Plan 9 from Outer Space* because of its reputation for being so bad it is good, the low-budget picture is, in fact, part of a little-known genre called lucha libre, or "free fight." In these movies, the flamboyant and colorful wrestlers fight the good fight against a wide array of villains, from gangsters to monsters.

> # Did You Know?
> The 1996 arcade video game *War Gods* features Anubis, guardian of the underworld.

Serious horror returned in 1967 with *The Mummy's Shroud*, another Hammer film in which actor Eddie Powell plays a revenge-seeking mummy. Today, the movie is best known for providing the featured ghoul a new set of duds. Rather than being draped in the traditional mummy suit of linen, Powell's cursed villain wears brown sackcloth. Also, unlike his slow-moving, shuffling forefathers, this one could chase his victims down without breaking a Cairo sweat.

Mummies Everywhere

While "Mummymania" at the movies appeared to be waning by the 1960s, its TV version exploded around this time thanks primarily to Universal's re-release of the many mummy movies from the 1930s, 1940s, and 1950s. Packaged to local television stations across the country as "Shock Theatre" or "Creature Features," the movie studio helped to introduce the mummy to a new generation of Americans.

Saturday morning cartoons also played this role. Cartoonists and animators had played with the mummy image since at least 1926.

In that year the popular comic duo of Mutt and Jeff costarred with a mummy in a silent short cartoon called *Mummy O'Mine*. By the 1960s, the mummy had become a staple of children's entertainment and was featured prominently in the popular *Scooby Doo* series. In the 1970s and 1980s, *The Groovie Goolies* and *Thundercats* were paid

Bubba Ho-Tep

One of strangest descendants of the mummy in popular culture is the independent film *Bubba Ho-Tep*. Based on a short story of the same name, the film combines "Ho-Tep," an ancient Egyptian surname, and "Bubba," a slang term for a male from the southern United States. Centered in a dilapidated retirement home in Texas, the film follows a sickly but living Elvis Presley and an African American friend who believes he is the assassinated president John F. Kennedy. The wacky premise, in which Elvis has switched his identity with one of many Elvis impersonators, also includes a long-dead mummy that returns to prey on the elderly residents until Elvis and JFK do something about it. The two buddies team up to take on the undead Egyptian, as JFK does some research and gets the lowdown on the soul-stealing mummy.

The final battle between the old men and the bandaged corpse is a campy delight, as jump-suit-wearing Elvis and the wheelchair-bound president struggle to send the monster back to its grave. More silly than scary, it gives new meaning to the Elvis classic "Burning Love." The movie's message is a poignant one. "This film is an ode to old people," says star Bruce Campbell. "It reflects something that's very true: older people in this society are invisible, and how quickly we forget." With the cult popularity of *Bubba Ho-Tep*, that message may just reach an audience.

Quoted in *Bubba Ho-Tep*, "The Making of *Bubba Ho-Tep*," MGM, 2003.

visits by the mummy too. And by 1997 the creature was popular enough to warrant the lead role in a series about reborn mummies called *Mummies Alive!*

The mummy found a natural fan club among preteen boys. Before long, the marketing of monster-themed toys and action figures became big business. Advertisers and marketers recognized the universal potential of mummy-themed products. In magazines, window displays, and on the Internet, mummies are everywhere. The image has been used to sell cigarettes, soda, beer, milk, pizza, and hundreds of other consumer goods. Says psychologist Carter Lupton: "Mummies have even become Christmas tree ornaments ranging from those emulating real coffins, to film mummies, to totally whimsical originals."[29] The image of the mummy that has appeared on puzzles, trading cards, clothing, and in songs, proved once and for all that the mummy was a pop culture icon extraordinaire.

Millennial Mummies

This iconic status was plucked again in novels like *The Eye of Horus* by Carol Thurston and R.L. Stine's *Goosebumps* series. In John Bellairs' 1983 novel *The Mummy, the Will, and the Crypt*, a 12-year-old boy named Johnny Dixon teams with a professor to battle the powerful forces of the supernatural. In the 1990 British film *Tales from the Darkside: The Movie*, the mummy figures in one episode set at a university and based on an Arthur Conan Doyle tale called "Lot No. 249."

In 1999, with the cantankerous cadaver being revived in so many forms, Universal Studios decided to get back into the mummy business. That year the studio released *The Mummy*, a special-effects spectacular starring Brendan Fraser and raven-haired beauty Rachel Weisz. Set in 1923 and directed by Stephen Sommers, the plot centers on a British librarian

> **Did You Know?**
>
> Christopher Lee's shaky mummy walk in 1959's *The Mummy* was no act; during the shoot he dislocated his shoulder and strained his back while breaking down a door on the set.

named Evelyn Carnahan, played by Weisz, who wants to conduct an archaeological dig at the ancient city of Hamunaptra. With the help of gung-ho adventurer Rick O'Connell, a man she saves from death, they begin their journey and are joined by Evelyn's brother Jonathan. The three are soon dismayed to find that another team of explorers has dreams of digging at the same spot. The rival group disturbs a long-buried tomb and unleashes a terrible curse. Rick and Evelyn are forced to defend themselves with shotguns and swords and destroy the curse once and for all. In this updated version, the mummy wears no bandages and comes and goes in a swirl of sand.

Audiences flocked to theaters to take in the special-effects spectacle. Critics, on the other hand, were divided. While some praised its spine-tingling storyline, others were left cold by this updated version of the classic horror film. "In the new *Mummy*, the cursed monster starts out as a glorified videogame effect, and then, when his flesh is restored, he radiates all the menace of a shaven-headed personal trainer," wrote critic Owen Gleiberman in 1999. "The walking-corpse gimmickry is fun . . . but, like the film, he leaves no haunting traces."[30]

Mummies rage in the special-effects spectacular The Mummy, *released by Universal Studios in 1999. The movie added a twist to previous big-screen portrayals in that the lead mummy wears no bandages and is eventually restored to its flesh-covered human state.*

Two years later *The Mummy Returns* did just that. With a larger budget—$100 million—the sequel powered to the top of the box office charts. Now, Evelyn and Rick are married and continue their archaeological work, with their eight-year-old son, Alex, tagging along. During their work they discover the Bracelet of Anubis, but High Priest Imhotep, newly back from the dead, seeks the bracelet to hatch a diabolical plan. Despite their mediocre reception by critics, *The Mummy* and its follow-up, *The Mummy Returns*, earned a combined $357 million at the US box office.

Mummy in China

One more follow-up, *The Mummy: Tomb of the Dragon Emperor*, was released in 2008. This time the producers enlarged the story and hired a new director, Rob Cohen. In the film, Rick and his wife, Evelyn, now played by Maria Bello, are asked to take an ancient diamond, the "Eye of Shangri-La," to China. The precious jewel has the magical ability to resurrect the Emperor Han, who was once cursed by a sorceress and, with his soldiers, turned into a phalanx of mummies. It can also lead the way to Shangri-La, pool of eternal life. Once in China, the explorer couple reunites with Alex, now grown, who has uncovered Han's tomb. An evil meddler, Professor Roger Wilson, tries to foil the three by bringing the dead emperor back to life and rushing to Shangri-La. The O'Connells must stop Wilson and the powerful Han before it is too late.

> **Did You Know?**
>
> Among the many mummy collectibles on the market is a 12-inch action figure featuring the original Boris Karloff character, which retails for nearly $300.

The intriguing premise of *The Mummy: Tomb of the Dragon Emperor* attracted a large audience and earned over $400 million at the worldwide box office. For Fraser, much of the film's success stemmed not from the eye-popping special effects but from the characters. "If you don't care about the people in the movie, then you're just watching a CGI [computer-generated image] exhibition. . . . In this case it's fathers and sons knocking skulls. . . . It's about searching for lost love. It's about reuniting a family, saving the world."[31]

Never Say Die

This latest series of mummy movies seemed to prove that the mummy cannot be stopped. Although not yet announced, a fourth installment is more than likely. The public's thirst for mummy stories continues unabated in the twenty-first century, millennia after the first people mummified their dead and prayed to their god to lead them to the afterlife.

Today, the mummy as monster remains a baffling and unpredictable creature. The folklore that has grown around it will likely remain popular as long as there are stories to be told. Mummy expert Zahi Hawass sees mummies and their stories as a window into the past that people can continue to learn from. "There must be a reason why mummies and tales of a distant past still resonate in our modern world," says Hawass. "The people buried . . . seem to speak to us from their graves, and I believe it can serve our own society if we listen to them."[32]

Source Notes

Chapter One: The Mummy as Monster

1. Quoted in Gregory William Mank, *Bela Lugosi and Boris Karloff: The Expanded Story of a Haunting Collaboration*. Jefferson, NC: McFarland, 2009, p. 128.
2. Quoted in *The Mummy*, Universal Legacy Series, DVD extras, 2009.
3. Quoted in Jason Jones, "*The Mummy* (1932)," Classic-Horror.com. October 9, 2002. http://classic-horror.com.
4. Quoted in Mank, *Bela Lugosi and Boris Karloff*, p. 133.
5. A.D.S., "*The Mummy* (1932): Life After 3,700 Years," review, *New York Times*, January 7, 1933. http://movies.nytimes.com.
6. A.D.S., "*The Mummy* (1932): Life After 3,700 Years."
7. Roger Ebert, "*The Mummy*," *Chicago Sun-Times*, May 7, 1999. www.rogerebert.com.
8. Howard Carter and A.C. Mace, *Tomb of Tutankhamen*. New York: Kessinger, 2003, p. 135.
9. Carter and Mace, *Tomb of Tutankhamen*, p. 141.
10. *New York Times*, "Times Man Views Splendors of Tomb of Tutankhamen," December 21, 1921, pp. 1–2.
11. Henry Field, *The Track of Man: Adventures of an Anthropologist*. New York: Greenwood, 1969, p. 43.

Chapter Two: Separating Mummy from Myth

12. Herodotus, "The Antiquity of Egypt," in *The Portable Greek Historians*, M.I. Finley, ed. New York: Penguin, 1977, p. 65.
13. Herodotus, "The Antiquity of Egypt," p. 69.
14. Quoted in "Why We Love Mummies," *Pittsburgh Tribune-Review*, July 31, 2008. www.pittsburghlive.com.
15. Quoted in Pyramid Power, "Curse of the Pharaohs," November 21, 2009. www.thepyramidpower.com.

16. Quoted in Zahi Hawass, *Valley of the Golden Mummies*. New York: Harry N. Abrams, 2000, p. 94.

17. Christine El Mahdy, *Mummies Myth and Magic*. London: Thames and Hudson, 1989, pp. 170–71.

18. W. Seipel, in *Human Mummies: A Global Survey of Their Status and the Techniques of Conservation*, edited by Konrad Spendler et al. New York: Springer, 1996, p. 4.

19. Heather Pringle, *The Mummy Congress*. New York: Fourth Estate, 2002, p. 193.

Chapter Three: Mummy Legends and Curses

20. Hawass, *Valley of the Golden Mummies*, p. 94.

21. Quoted in Hawass, *Valley of the Golden Mummies*, pp. 94–95.

22. Hawass, *Valley of the Golden Mummies*, p. 97.

23. Jasmine Day, *The Mummy's Curse: Mummymania in the English-Speaking World*. New York: Taylor & Francis, 2006, p. 50.

24. Margaret Alice Murray, *My First Hundred Years*. London: W. Kimber, 1963, p. 176.

25. Quoted in Rebecca Shokrian, "Secrets of 'The Mummy Road Show' Unraveled," National Geographic News, March 27, 2002. http://news.nationalgeographic.com.

Chapter Four: The Mummy and Popular Culture

26. Mark Twain, *The Innocents Abroad: Roughing It*. New York: Library of America, p. 505.

27. Quoted in William Tait and Christian Isobel Johnstone, eds., "Loudon's Legacy to Gardeners," *Tait's Edinburgh Magazine*, vol. 1, 1834, p. 190.

28. Bram Stoker, *The Jewel of Seven Stars*. New York: Harper & Brothers, 1904; Google eBook, pp. 226–27.

29. Carter Lupton, "'Mummymania'" for the Masses—Is Egyptology Cursed by the Mummy's Curse?," *Consuming Ancient Egypt*. Sussex, UK: Psychology Press, p. 40.

30. Owen Gleiberman, "*The Mummy*," *Entertainment Weekly*, May 14, 1999. www.ew.com.

31. Brendan Fraser, "Brendan Fraser Interview—*Mummy: Tomb of the Dragon Emperor*," video, About.com: Hollywood Movies, 2008. http://video.about.com.

32. Hawass, *Valley of the Golden Mummies*, p. 97.

For Further Exploration

Books

Eva von Dassow, *The Egyptian Book of the Dead*. New York: Chronicle Books, 2008.

Francis Janot and Zahi Hawass, *The Royal Mummies: Immortality in Ancient Egypt*. New York: White Star, 2008.

J.P. Mallory, *The Tarim Mummies*. London: Thames and Hudson, 2008.

Richard Sugg, *Mummies, Cannibals, and Vampires: The History of Corpse Medicine from the Renaissance to the Victorians*. New York: Routledge, 2011.

Alfried Wieczorek and Wilfried Rosendahl, *Mummies of the World*. New York: Prestel USA, 2010.

Websites

The British Museum (www.ancientegypt.co.uk/menu.html). One of the world's foremost mummy collections is housed in London's British Museum. This informative website discusses life in ancient Egypt, the gods and goddesses worshipped at the time, and mummification. Chock-full of creepy and dramatic pictures, the site also provides a step-by-step visual trip through embalming and wrapping.

Classic-Horror.com (http://classic-horror.com/reviews/mummy_1932). For a cinematic trip down "mummery" lane, visit this tribute site. The history of Karloff's 1932 classic and its subsequent knock-offs are explored. Each page contains an in-depth look at the chosen movie.

Boris Karloff (www.karloff.com). Karloff played the mummy in the 1932 film, and now, after his death, he is a small industry. This site provides information about the classically trained actor's life beyond horror films. It includes his family tree, along with the opportunity to view artists' portraits of Karloff. The site is maintained by Sara Karloff, the actor's daughter.

Monster Mummies of Japan (http://pinktentacle.com/2009/03/ monster-mummies-of-japan). This odd little site pays tribute to the mummified remains of what it calls Japan's demons, mermaids, and monks.

Mummies of the World (www.mummiesoftheworld.com). This website is a companion to the touring show of the same name. Here, the curious can read up on mummy science, look at a preview of the exhibition, and find out what makes mummification a worldwide phenomenon.

Mummy Tombs (www.mummytombs.com/main.quiz.htm). This website includes historical facts and how-to sections that provide instructions on how to make a mummy.

Index

Note: Boldface page numbers indicate illustrations.

Picture Credits

About the Author

David Robson's many books for young people include *Cyclops*, *Encounters with Vampires*, and *The Devil*. He is also an award-winning playwright whose work for the stage has been performed across the country and abroad. He lives with his family in Wilmington, Delaware.